# 6

# american popular piano

## ETUDES

**Compositions by**
## Christopher Norton

**Additional Compositions and Arrangements**
## Dr. Scott McBride Smith

**Editor**
## Dr. Scott McBride Smith

**Associate Editor**
## Clarke MacIntosh

**Music**

**Book Design & Engraving**
Andrew Jones

**Cover Design**
Wagner Design

# A Note about this Book

Pop music styles can be grouped into three broad categories:

- **lyrical** — pieces with a beautiful singing quality and rich harmonies; usually played at a slow tempo;

- **rhythmic** — more up-tempo pieces, with energetic, catchy rhythms; these often have a driving left hand part;

- **ensemble** — works meant to be played with other musicians, or with backing tracks (or both!); this type of piece requires careful listening and shared energy.

**American Popular Piano** has been deliberately designed to develop skills in all three areas.

You can integrate the cool, motivating pieces in **American Popular Piano** into your piano studies in several ways.

- pick a piece you like and learn it; when you're done, pick another!

- choose a piece from each category to develop a complete range of skills in your playing;

- polish a particular favorite for your local festival or competition. Works from **American Popular Piano** are featured on the lists of required pieces for many festivals and competitions;

- use the pieces as optional contemporary selections in music examinations;

- Or...just have fun!

Going hand-in-hand with the repertoire in **American Popular Piano** are the innovative **Etudes Albums** and **Skills Books,** designed to enhance each student's musical experience by building technical and aural skills.

- **Technical Etudes** in both Classical and Pop Styles are based on musical ideas and technical challenges drawn from the repertoire. Practice these to improve your chops!

- **Improvisation Etudes** offer an exciting new approach to improvisation that guides students effortlessly into spontaneous creativity. Not only does the user-friendly module structure integrate smoothly into traditional lessons, it opens up a whole new understanding of the repertoire being studied.

- **Skills Books** help students develop key supporting skills in sight-reading, ear-training and technique; presented in complementary study modules that are both practical and effective.

Use all of the elements of **American Popular Piano** together to incorporate a comprehensive course of study into your everyday routine. The carefully thought-out pacing makes learning almost effortless. Making music and real progress has never been so much fun!

**Library and Archives Canada Cataloguing in Publication**

Norton, Christopher, 1953-

American popular piano [music] : etudes / compositions by Christopher Norton ;
additional compositions and arrangements, Scott McBride Smith ;
editor, Scott McBride Smith ; associate editor, Clarke MacIntosh.

To be complete in 11 volumes.
Publisher's nos.: APP E-00 (Level P); APP E-01 (Level 1); APP E-02 (Level 2); APP E-03 (Level 3); APP E-04 (Level 4); APP E-05 (Level 5).
Contents: Level P -- Level 1 -- Level 2 -- Level 3 -- Level 4 -- Level 5.
Miscellaneous information: The series is organized in 11 levels, from preparatory to level 10, each including a repertoire album,
an etudes album, a skills book, a "technic" book, and an instrumental backings compact disc.

ISBN 1-897379-11-0 (level P).--ISBN 1-897379-12-9 (level 1).--ISBN 1-897379-13-7 (level 2).--ISBN 1-897379-14-5 (level 3).--
ISBN 1-897379-15-3 (level 4).--ISBN 1-897379-16-1 (level 5).--ISBN 978-1-897379-11-0 (level P).--ISBN 978-1-897379-12-7 (level 1).--
ISBN 978-1-897379-13-4 (level 2).--ISBN 978-1-897379-14-1 (level 3).--ISBN 978-1-897379-15-8 (level 4).--ISBN 978-1-897379-16-5 (level 5).--
ISBN 978-1-897379-17-2 (level 6).--ISBN 978-1-897379-18-9 (level 7).--ISBN 978-1-897379-19-6 (level 8)

1. Piano--Studies and exercises. I. Smith, Scott McBride II. MacIntosh, S. Clarke, 1959- III. Title. IV. Title: Études

MT222.N884 2006                    786.2                    C2006-906214-5

# LEVEL 6 ETUDES

# Table of Contents

# Improv Etude - Bowling Green

**Module 1**

### Concept: root position & first inversions

A triad is a three note chord. A **root position triad** in **close position** is written line-line-line or space-space-space. A chord takes its name from the bottom note of the chord in root position, called the **root**.

Triads may also be written in **first inversion**. In a first inversion triad, the third of the chord is on the bottom.

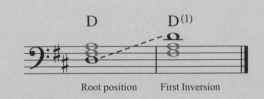

One way to change a root position triad to first inversion is to take the root off the bottom and put it on top.

---

**A** Label the first inversion triads with their lettername. Also add a bracketed 1 to indicate "first inversion". Practice the left hand first *without*, then *with* the backing track.

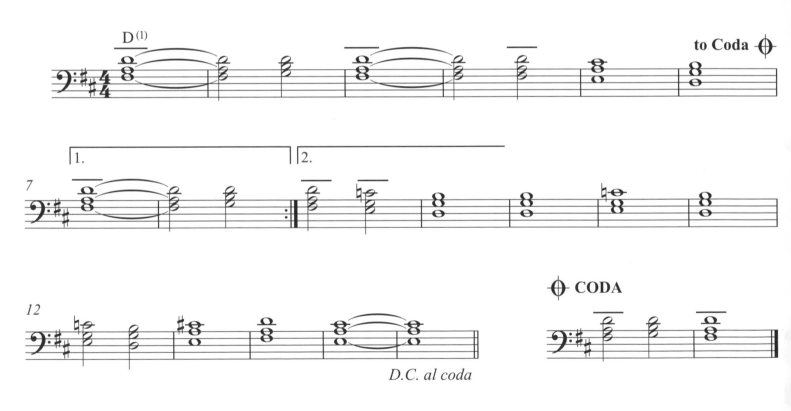

*D.C. al coda*

---

**B** Tap this rhythm while counting out loud; repeat until memorized. Then tap the rhythm with your right hand while playing the chord progression with your left. Finally, make up your own rhythms to go with the left hand chord progression.

## Improv Tools

Improvisations often use scale-based ideas. To improvise on *Bowling Green*, you will use an Improv Notes Set based on the **A Mixolydian mode**.

One way to describe A Mixolydian is as an A Major scale with a G♮ instead of a G♯. Lowering the 7th degree of any major scale by a half step changes it into a Mixolydian mode.

There are specific Improv Tools you can use to make your scale-based improvisation interesting and musical.

**Idea & Variation**: play a scale-based idea and then repeat it slightly varied (even by as little as one note!):

**Grace Notes**: grace notes can add real expressiveness and sophistication to your improvisation. Imagine a vocalist or guitar player "bending" a note:

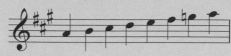

A Mixolydian mode

**C** Using the Improv Notes Set as indicated in the score, play various right hand improvisations. Use the Improv Tools, above, to get started. Practice *with* the backing track.

Set A
Improv notes:

Improvisation
**Set A** Improv Notes
**to Coda**

*D.C. al coda*

**4**

**D** Now improvise hands together. Practice first *without*, then *with* the backing track.

*D.C. al coda*

✔ **Improv Tip:** *Try to be expressive when you improvise. Don't just play a bland series of notes; make each one really count in establishing a certain mood.*

## Vamping Tools

Vamping is an improvised accompaniment style. It often features repeated patterns based on blocked chords or broken chords in the right hand against single notes in the left hand. You can vary right hand chords in several ways:

Vamp Idea 1 – a syncopated rhythm, followed by on-beat chords:

Idea 2 – repeat a syncopated pattern:

Idea 3 – alternate with a more complex syncopated rhythm:

**E** Vamp various right hand accompaniments using the chords [in brackets] indicated below. Use the Vamping Tools above to get started. Practice first *without*, then *with* the backing track.

*D.C. al coda*

# Improv Etude - Bowling Green

**Module 2**

## Concept: second inversions

Remember that a triad is a three note chord. A **root position triad** in **close position** is written line-line-line or space-space-space. A chord takes its name from the bottom note of the chord in **root position**, called the **root**.

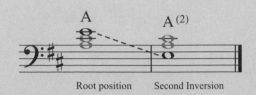

Chords may also be written in **second inversion**. A second inversion triad has the fifth of the chord on the bottom.

One way to change a root position triad to second inversion is to take the top note and move it to the bottom.

**A** Label the second inversion triads with their lettername and a bracketed 2 for "second inversion". Practice the left hand first *without*, then *with* the backing track.

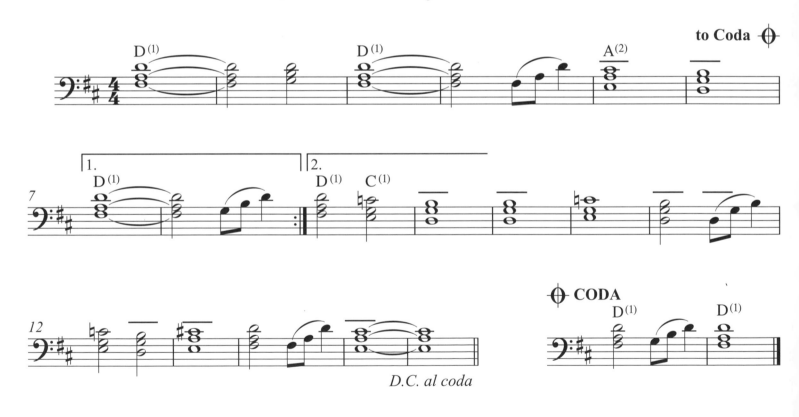

*D.C. al coda*

**B** Tap this rhythm while counting out loud; repeat until memorized. Then tap the rhythm with your right hand while playing the chord progression with your left. Finally, make up your own rhythms to go with the left hand chord progression.

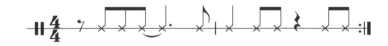

## Improv Tools

Improvisations can also use arpeggio-based ideas.

**Grace Notes**: add "drops" of interest to your improvisation with the occassional use of grace notes:

**Idea & Variation**: play an arpeggio-based idea and then repeat it with a slight variation:

**Rhythmic Shift**: play an arpeggio-based idea and then repeat it starting on a different beat:

**C** Using the Improv Notes Set as indicated in the score, play various right hand improvisations. Use the Improv Tools, above and in the previous Module, to get started. Practice *with* the backing track.

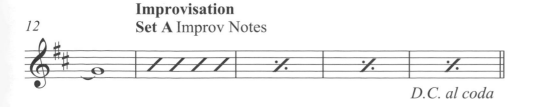

*D.C. al coda*

**8**

D Now improvise hands together. Practice first *without*, then *with* the backing track.

**Improv Tip:** *Try alternating Improv Tools; for example, use **Rhythmic Shift** followed by **Grace Notes**.*

## Vamping Tools

Vamps can also use broken chords in the right hand. You can create interest by varying the starting note of the arpeggio.

Idea 2 – start from the top note of the chord:

Vamp Idea 1 – start from the bottom note of the chord:

Idea 3 – start from the middle note of the chord:

**E** Vamp various right hand accompaniments using the chords [in brackets] indicated below. Use the Vamping Tools, above and in the previous Module, to get started. Practice first *without*, then *with* the backing track.

*D.C. al coda*

# Improv Etude - Bowling Green

**Module 3**

### Concept: split chords

**Split chords** can occur when playing chords with both hands. A split chord has a bass note in the left hand that is not the root of the chord – sometimes it is not a note from the chord at all.

For example, in m.14 of the Vamp on page 13, you will see a D chord in first inversion in the right hand with an A as the bass note in the left hand. This is a split chord, written D/A, where the "/" is used to indicate first the chord in the right hand and then the bass note in the left hand. Here are two examples of split chords. Both

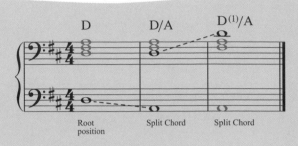

would be called "D over A".

In the *Bowling Green* improvisation, the bass note of the split chords is played in the backing track, creating a split chord sound in relation to the left hand chord.

**A** Label the split chords with their lettername (e.g., G/D, C/G, or D/A) and bracketed 1 for the right hand inversion, where appropriate. Practice the left hand first *without*, then *with* the backing track.

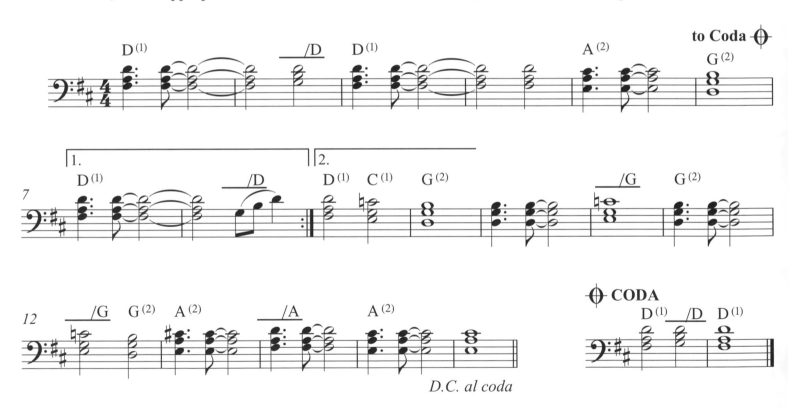

*D.C. al coda*

**B** Tap this rhythm while counting out loud; repeat until memorized. Then tap the rhythm with your right hand while playing the chord progression with your left. Finally, make up your own rhythms to go with the left hand chord progression.

## Improv Tools

There are other Improv Tools you can use to add color and interest to your improvisation. These Tools can be used with either scale-based or arpeggio-based ideas.

**Pedal Notes**: a pedal note is a held or repeated note that doesn't change when the melody moves. Here, the A's are pedal notes "above" the melody:

**Thirds**: create melodies that can be harmonized in thirds:

**Direction Change**: create an idea that goes up, then down – or down, then up:

C  Using the Improv Notes Set as indicated in the score, play various right hand improvisations. Use the Improv Tools, above and in the previous Modules, to get started. Practice *with* the backing track.

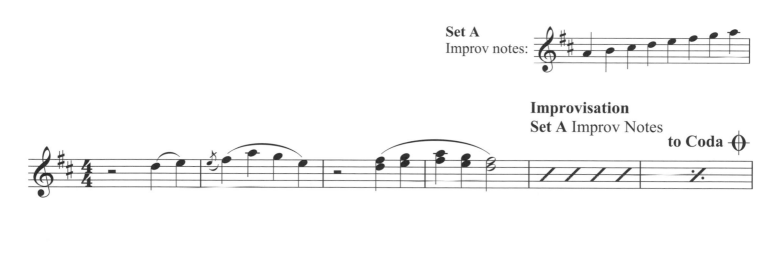

*D.C. al coda*

12

**D** Now improvise hands together. Practice first *without*, then *with* the backing track.

## Vamping Tools

You can use a mix of blocked and broken chords in your vamp.

**Vamp Idea 1** – syncopated blocked chords followed by a simple arpeggio:

Idea 2 – a more noticeable use of the arpeggio:

Idea 3 – even more arpeggios:

**E** Vamp various right hand accompaniments using the chords [in brackets] indicated below. Use the Vamping Tools, above and in the previous Modules, to get started. Practice first *without*, then *with* the backing track.

*D.C. al coda*

# Improv Etude - Heavy Footed

**Module 1**

### Concept: Dominant 7 chords

A **Dominant 7 chord** (also known as a 7 chord) combines a major triad (e.g., C-E-G) with a minor 7th above the root (e.g., B♭). Sometimes this is done using all four notes (e.g., C-E-G-B♭), but often it is done with only three notes to achieve the same sound.

7 chords may be written in **first inversion**. In a first inversion 7 chord, the third of the chord is on the bottom. One way to change a root position 7 chord to

first inversion is to take the root off the bottom and put it on top. When only three notes are used to play a first inversion 7 chord, it is usual to omit the 5th of the chord.

**A** Label the first inversion 7 chords with their lettername (e.g., C7) and a bracketed 1 for "first inversion". Practice the left hand first *without*, then *with* the backing track.

**B** Tap this rhythm while counting out loud; repeat until memorized. Then tap the rhythm with your right hand while playing the chord progression with your left. Finally, make up your own rhythms to go with the left hand chord progression.

## Improv Tools

Improvisations often make use of licks. **Licks** are short, catchy musical ideas – like **motifs**.

To improvise on *Heavy Footed*, you will use the **F Blues scale**. One way to describe the F Blues scale is as an F **minor pentatonic** (F, A♭, B♭, C, E♭) with an added lowered 5th scale degree (C♭).

**F Blues scale**

There are various Improv Tools you can use to make your improvisation interesting and musical.

**Idea & Variation**: play a lick and then repeat it with a slight variation:

**Grace Notes**: add grace notes to your lick to achieve a sophisticated, professional effect. Imagine a vocalist or guitar player "bending" a note:

**C** Using the Improv Notes Set as indicated in the score, play various right hand improvisations. Use the Improv Tools, above, to get started. Practice *with* the backing track.

**Set A**
Improv notes:

**Improvisation**
**Set A** Improv Notes

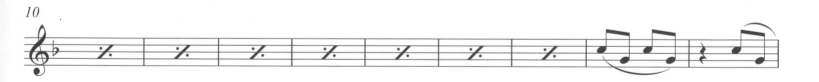

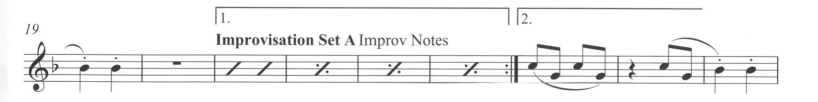

**Improvisation**
**Set A** Improv Notes

**D** Now improvise hands together. Practice first *without*, then *with* the backing track.

✔ **Improv Tip:** *Leave rests between your phrases occasionally, as though you are a wind player taking breaths.*

## Vamping Tools

Vamps sometimes use **riffs** – melodic, harmonic, or rhythmic **ostinato** patterns that form the basis of a piece – such as the bass line in *Heavy Footed*. When the left hand part is busy, the right hand can be simpler, using different rhythms to create interest.

Right hand rhythmic pattern 1:

Right hand rhythmic pattern 2:

Right hand rhythmic pattern 3:

**E** Vamp various right hand accompaniments using the chords [in brackets] indicated below. Use the Vamping Tools, above, to get started. Practice first *without*, then *with* the backing track.

# Improv Etude - Heavy Footed

**Module 2**

### Concept: Dominant 7 chords

A **Dominant 7 chord** (also known as a 7 chord) combines a major triad (e.g., F-A-C) with a minor 7th above the root (e.g., E♭). Sometimes this is done using all four notes (e.g., F-A-C-E♭), but often it is done with only three notes to achieve the same sound.

7 chords may be written in **third inversion**. In a third inversion 7 chord, the minor seventh of the chord is on the bottom. One way to change a root position 7 chord to

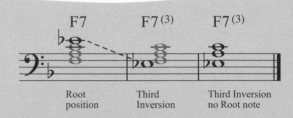

third inversion is to take the minor 7th off the top and put it on the bottom. When only three notes are used to play a third inversion 7 chord, the root is usually omitted.

**A** Label the third inversion 7 chords with their lettername (e.g., F7) and a bracketed 3 for "third inversion". Practice the left hand first *without*, then *with* the backing track.

**B** Tap this rhythm while counting out loud; repeat until memorized. Then tap the rhythm with your right hand while playing the chord progression with your left. Finally, make up your own rhythms to go with the left hand chord progression.

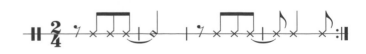

## Improv Tools

Another Improv Tool you can use is **Call & Response**, in addition to **Idea & Variation** and **Grace Notes**.

**Grace Notes**: a great way to "spice up" your improvisation:

**Idea & Variation**: play an idea and, using essentially the same notes, play it again with a slight change:

**Call & Response**: play an idea and then "answer" it with a contrasting idea:

**C** Using the Improv Notes Set as indicated in the score, play various right hand improvisations. Use the Improv Tools, above and in the previous Module, to get started. Practice *with* the backing track.

Set A
Improv notes:

**Improvisation**
**Set A** Improv Notes

*10*

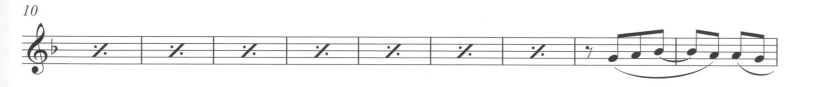

*19*

**Improvisation Set A** Improv Notes

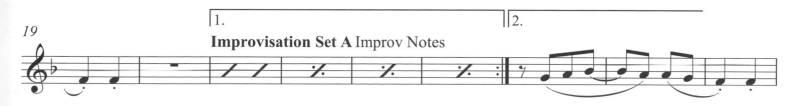

*24*

**Improvisation**
**Set A** Improv Notes

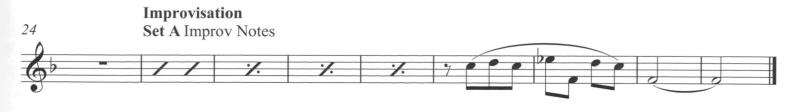

**D** Now improvise hands together. Practice first *without*, then *with* the backing track.

**Improv Tip:** *Try inventing a new idea for each section of your improvisation.*

## Vamping Tools

The Vamp can also use figures in the right hand which complement the bass riff.

Idea 2 – the same figure with a grace note added:

Vamp Idea 1 – a figure in thirds:

Idea 3 – a figure using pedal notes above the melody:

**E** Vamp various accompaniments using the chords [in brackets] indicated below. Use the Vamping Tools, above and in the previous Module, to get started. Practice first *without*, then *with* the backing track.

# Improv Etude - Heavy Footed

**Module 3**

## Concept: 9 chords

A **9 chord** is a **7 chord** with the 9th scale degree added. Sometimes this is done using all five notes – a major triad (e.g., Bb-D-F) with the minor 7th (e.g., Ab) and major 9th (e.g., C) added (e.g., Bb-D-F-Ab-C) – or sometimes it is done with only three notes to achieve the same sound.

9 chords may be written in **first inversion**. In a first inversion 9 chord, the third of the chord is on the bottom. One way to change a root position 9 chord to

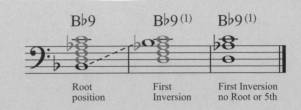

first inversion is to take the root off the bottom and put it up an octave to be the second note from the top – just underneath the 9th.

In the *Heavy Footed* improvisation, the "Bb" bass note is played in the backing track. In the Vamp, on page 25, you play it in your left hand.

**A** Label the 9 chords with their lettername (e.g., Bb9) and a bracketed 1 for "first inversion". Practice the left hand first *without*, then *with* the backing track.

**B** Tap this rhythm while counting out loud; repeat until memorized. Then tap the rhythm with your right hand while playing the chord progression with your left. Finally, make up your own rhythms to go with the left hand chord progression.

## Improv Tools

There are various other things you can use to "spice up" your improvisation.

**Idea & Variation**: play an idea and, using essentially the same notes, play it again with a change of direction:

**Pedal Notes**: a pedal note is a repeated note that doesn't change when the melody moves. Here, the F's are pedal notes "above" the melody– using a grace note, too:

**Tremolo**: try this very "bluesy" effect:

**C**  Using the Improv Notes Set as indicated in the score, play various right hand improvisations. Use the Improv Tools, above and in the previous Modules, to get started. Practice *with* the backing track.

**Set A**
Improv notes:

**Improvisation**
**Set A** Improv Notes

10

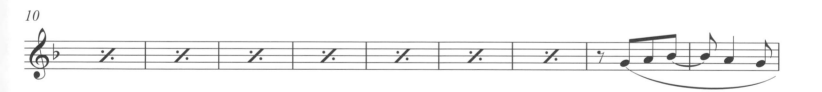

19

**Improvisation**
**Set A** Improv Notes

24

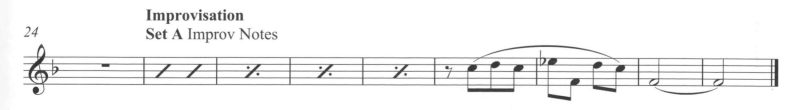

**24**

D Now improvise hands together. Practice first *without*, then *with* the backing track.

✔ **Improv Tip:** *Another way to use rests is to use them to delay the main beat. Choose a spot where you were going to play on beat 1. Instead, put a rest there and bring the note in a bit late.*

## Vamping Tools

Now try vamping with a busier bass riff. Your right hand can use a combination of chords and independent figures to make an interesting vamp.

Vamp Idea 1 – a calm right hand rhythmic pattern:

Idea 2 – substitute a figure in thirds for contrast:

Idea 3 –a figure using pedal notes above throughout:

**E**  Vamp various accompaniments using the chords [in brackets] indicated below. Use the Vamping Tools, above and in the previous Modules, to get started. Practice first *without*, then *with* the backing track.

# Improv Etude - Clean Sweep

**Module 1**

### Concept: Dominant 7 chords

A **Dominant 7 chord** (also known as a 7 chord) combines a major triad (e.g., E-G♯-B) with a minor 7th above the root (e.g., D). Sometimes this is done using all four notes (e.g., E-G♯-B-D), but often it is done with only three notes to achieve the same sound.

7 chords may be written in **first inversion**. In a first inversion 7 chord, the third of the chord is on the bottom. One way to change a root position 7 chord to

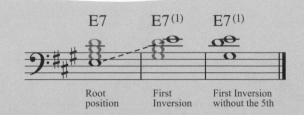

first inversion is to take the root off the bottom and put it on top. When only three notes are used to play a first inversion 7 chord, it is usual to omit the 5th of the chord.

**A** Label the first inversion 7 chords with their lettername (e.g., E7) and a bracketed 1 for "first inversion". Practice the left hand first *without*, then *with* the backing track.

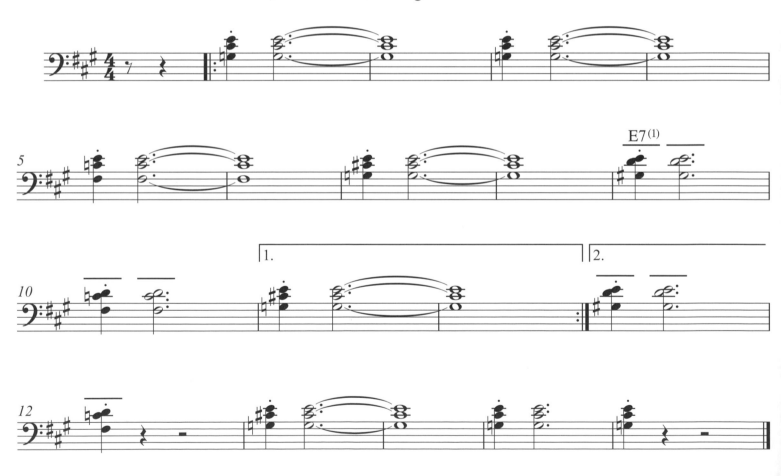

**B** Tap this rhythm while counting out loud; repeat until memorized. Then tap the rhythm with your right hand while playing the chord progression with your left. Finally, make up your own rhythms to go with the left hand chord progression.

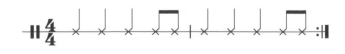

## Improv Tools

To improvise on *Clean Sweep*, you will use the **A Blues scale**.

One way to describe the A Blues scale is as an A **minor pentatonic** (A, C, D, E, G) with an added lowered 5th scale degree (E♭).

**A Blues scale**

There are Improv Tools you can use to make your improvisation more interesting and musical.

**Call & Response**: think of an idea, then "answer" it with a contrasting idea:

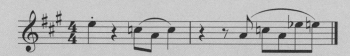

**Rhythmic Shift**: play an arpeggio-based idea and then re-state it starting on a different beat in the bar:

**C** Using the Improv Notes Set as indicated in the score, play various right hand improvisations. Use the Improv Tools, above, to get started. Practice *with* the backing track.

**28**

**D** Now improvise hands together. Practice first *without*, then *with* the backing track.

✔ **Improv Tip:** *A short melodic idea can be repeated several times.  Make it fresh by shifting accents or inserting rests.*

## Vamping Tools

Vamping is an improvised accompaniment, often with chords in the right hand against single notes in the left. Vamps can also use **riffs**, such as the bass line in *Clean Sweep*. When the left hand part is busy, the right hand can be simpler, using rhythmic patterns to create interest.

Right hand rhythmic pattern 1:

Right hand rhythmic pattern 2:

Right hand rhythmic pattern 3:

**E** Vamp various right hand accompaniments using the chords [in brackets] indicated below. Use the Vamping Tools, above, to get started. Practice first *without*, then *with* the backing track.

# Improv Etude - Clean Sweep

**Module 2**

## Concept: Dominant 7 chords

A **Dominant 7 chord** (also known as a 7 chord) combines a major triad (e.g., A-C♯-E) with a minor 7th above the root (e.g., G♮). Sometimes this is done using all four notes (e.g., A-C♯-E-G♮), but often it is done with only three notes to achieve the same sound.

7 chords may be written in **third inversion**. In a third inversion 7 chord, the minor seventh of the chord is on the bottom. One way to change a root position 7 chord

to third inversion is to take the 7th off the top and put it on bottom. When only three notes are used to play a third inversion 7 chord, it is usual to omit the root.

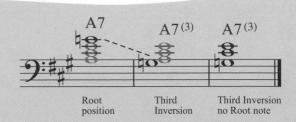

**A** Label the third inversion 7 chords with their lettername (e.g., A7) and a bracketed 3 for "third inversion". Practice the left hand first *without*, then *with* the backing track.

**B** Tap this rhythm while counting out loud; repeat until memorized. Then tap the rhythm with your right hand while playing the chord progression with your left. Finally, make up your own rhythms to go with the left hand chord progression.

## Improv Tools

**Pedal Notes** is another Improv Tool you can use, in addition to **Call & Response** and **Rhythmic Shift**.

**Call & Response**: one idea "answered" by another:

**Rhythmic Shift**: play a scale-based idea, then re-state it starting on a different beat:

**Pedal Notes**: a pedal note is a repeated note that doesn't change when the melody moves. Here the A's are pedal notes "above":

**C** Using the Improv Notes Set as indicated in the score, play various right hand improvisations. Use the Improv Tools, above and in the previous Module, to get started. Practice *with* the backing track.

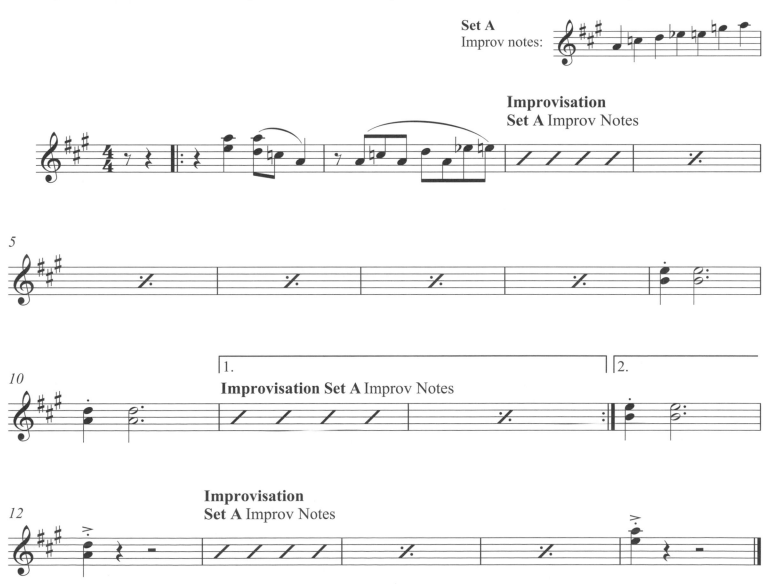

**D** Now improvise hands together. Practice first *without*, then *with* the backing track.

**✔ Improv Tip:** *Rhythm is an important part of your improv. Try to contrast short and long note values.*

## Vamping Tools

The bass **riff** in *Clean Sweep* can also be varied to create interest. Here are three more vamp ideas that complement a "jucier" bass riff.

Right hand rhythmic pattern 1:

Right hand rhythmic pattern 2:

Right hand rhythmic pattern 3:

**E** Vamp various accompaniments using the chords [in brackets] indicated below. Use the Vamping Tools, above and in the previous Module, to get started. Practice first *without*, then *with* the backing track.

# Improv Etude - Clean Sweep

**Module 3**

### Concept: 9 chords

A **9 chord** is a **7 chord** with the 9th scale degree added. Sometimes this is done using all five notes – a major triad (e.g., D-F♯-A) with the minor 7th (e.g., C♮) and major 9th (e.g., E) added (e.g., D-F♯-A-C♮-E) – or sometimes it is done with only three notes to achieve the same sound.

9 chords may be written in **first inversion**. In a first inversion 9 chord, the third of the chord is on the bottom. One way to change a root position 9 chord to

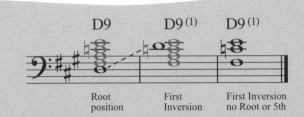

first inversion is to take the root off the bottom and put it up an octave to be the second note from the top – just underneath the 9th.

For improvising on *Clean Sweep*, the 5th and root will be left out.

**A** Label the first inversion 9 chords with their lettername (e.g., D9) and a bracketed 1 for "first inversion". Practice the left hand first *without*, then *with* the backing track.

**B** Tap this rhythm while counting out loud; repeat until memorized. Then tap the rhythm with your right hand while playing the chord progression with your left. Finally, make up your own rhythms to go with the left hand chord progression.

## Improv Tools

There are other Improv Tools you can use to make your improvisation ideas more interesting and musical.

**Idea & Variation**: think of an idea and, using essentially the same notes, play it again with a slight change:

**Grace Notes**: "spice up" your improvisation with grace notes – try to keep them short and light:

**Tremolos**: often used by blues players, experiment with playing them fast or slow to see which works for you:

**C**  Using the Improv Notes Set as indicated in the score, play various right hand improvisations. Use the Improv Tools, above and in the previous Modules, to get started. Practice *with* the backing track.

**36**

**D** Now improvise hands together. Practice first *without*, then *with* the backing track.

Set A
Improv notes:

**Improv Tip:** *Try playing the same melody with different chords and listen to the effect.*

## Vamping Tools

Now try using an even busier bass **riff**. The right hand part can stay quite calm to blend with the bass line running continuously throughout the vamp.

Vamp Idea 1:

Vamp Idea 2:

Vamp Idea 3:

**E** Vamp various accompaniments using the chords [in brackets] indicated below. Use the Vamping Tools, above and in the previous Modules, to get started. Practice first *without*, then *with* the backing track.

# Improv Etude - Happy Times

**Module 1**

### Review: Dominant 7 chords & inversions

A **Dominant 7 chord** (also known as a 7 chord) combines a major triad with a minor 7th above the root. Sometimes this is done using all four notes (the triad plus the minor 7th), but often it is done with only three notes to achieve the same sound.

7 chords may be written in **first** or **third inversion**. In a first inversion 7 chord, the third of the chord is on the bottom. In a third inversion 7 chord, the minor

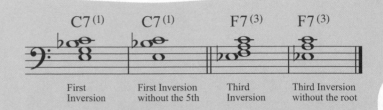

seventh of the chord is on the bottom. To review changing root position 7 chords to first inversion or third inversion and three-note voicings, see Modules 1 & 2 of *Heavy Footed* (pp. 14 & 18) and *Clean Sweep* (pp. 26 & 30).

**A** Label the third inversion 7 chords with their lettername (e.g., F7) and a bracketed 3 for "third inversion". Practice the left hand first *without*, then *with* the backing track.

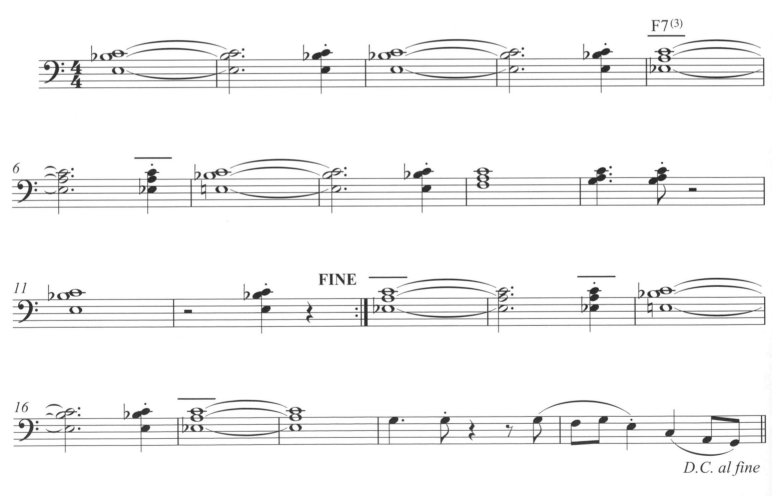

**B** Tap this rhythm while counting out loud; repeat until memorized. Then tap the rhythm with your right hand while playing the chord progression with your left. Finally, make up your own rhythms to go with the left hand chord progression.

## Improv Tools

Improvisations can make use of licks. **Licks** are short, catchy musical ideas – like **motifs**.

To improvise on *Happy Times*, you will use the **C Blues scale**. One way to describe the C Blues scale is as a C **minor pentatonic** (C, E♭, F, G, B♭) with an added lowered 5th scale degree (G♭).

There are Improv Tools you can use to make your improvisation interesting and musical.

**Rhythmic Shift**: play a lick and then restate it starting on a different beat in the bar:

**C Blues scale**

**Grace Notes**: make your melodies more characterful with careful use of grace notes:

**C** Using the Improv Notes Set as indicated in the score, play various right hand improvisations. Use the Improv Tools, above, to get started. Practice *with* the backing track.

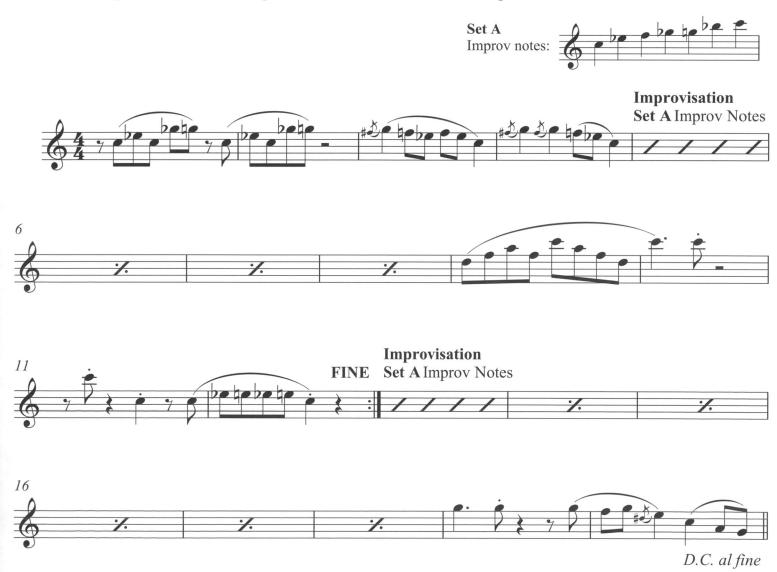

*D.C. al fine*

**40**

**D** Now improvise hands together. Practice first *without*, then *with* the backing track.

## Vamping Tools

Vamping is an improvised accompaniment, often with chords in the right hand against single notes in the left. *Happy Times* has a **calypso** feel with the rhythmic pattern in the bass and the simple syncopations in the right hand.

Right hand rhythmic pattern 1:

Right hand rhythmic pattern 2:

Right hand rhythmic pattern 3:

**E** Vamp various right hand accompaniments using the chords [in brackets] indicated below. Use the Vamping Tools, above, to get started. Practice first *without*, then *with* the backing track.

*D.C. al fine*

# Improv Etude - Happy Times

**Module 2**

## Concept: minor 7 chords

A **minor 7 chord (m7)** combines a minor triad (e.g., D-F-A) with a minor 7th above the root (e.g., C). Notice this is the same construction as the 7 chord, only based on a minor triad. Sometimes this is done using all four notes (e.g., D-F-A-C), but often it is done using only three notes to achieve the same sound.

Minor 7 chords may be written in **first inversion**. As with 7 chords, one way to change a root position m7

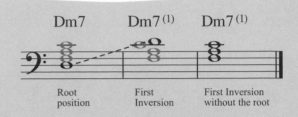

chord to first inversion is to take the root off the bottom and put it on top.

In the *Happy Times* improvisation, the "D" bass note is played in the backing track. In the Vamp, on page 45, you play it in your left hand.

**A** Label the first inversion 7 and m7 chords with their lettername (e.g., C7 or Dm7) and a bracketed 1 for "first inversion". Practice the left hand first *without*, then *with* the backing track.

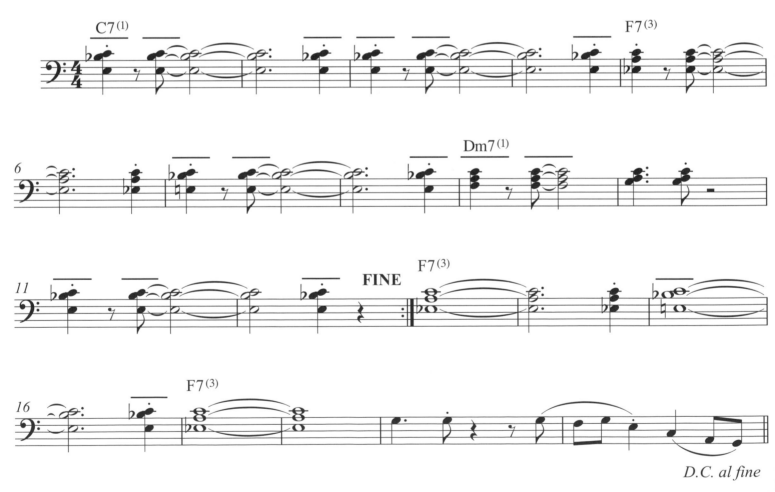

**B** Tap this rhythm while counting out loud; repeat until memorized. Then tap the rhythm etuh your right hand while playing the chord progression with your left. Finally, make up your own rhythms to go with the left hand chord progression.

## Improv Tools

**Call & Response** is another Improv Tool you can use, in addition to the **Rhythmic Shift** and **Grace Notes**.

**Grace Notes**: these remain a staple for "spicing up" your improvisation in many styles:

**Rhythmic Shift**: play an idea and then restate it starting on a different beat in the bar:

**Call & Response**: play an idea, then "answer" it with another:

C Using the Improv Notes Set as indicated in the score, play various right hand improvisations. Use the Improv Tools, above and in the previous Module, to get started. Practice *with* the backing track.

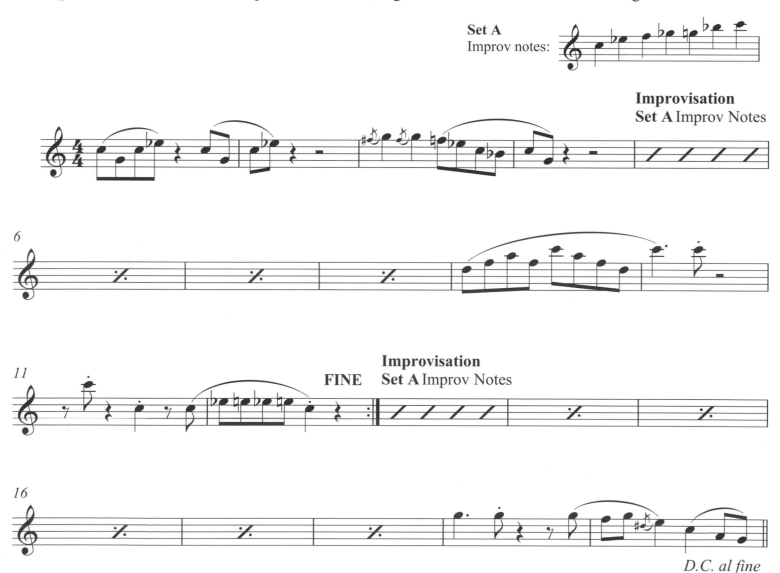

*D.C. al fine*

**D** Now improvise hands together. Practice first *without*, then *with* the backing track.

**Improv Tip:** *Don't be afraid to use "blue" notes (♭3, ♭5, ♭7) to make your melody expressive in this style.*

## Vamping Tools

Here are three more ideas for your vamp, using broken chords, that complement the bass **riff** running throughout *Happy Times*.

Vamp Idea 1:

Idea 2:

Idea 3:

**E** Vamp various right hand accompaniments using the chords [in brackets] indicated below. Use the Vamping Tools, above and in the previous Module, to get started. Practice first *without*, then *with* the backing track.

*D.C. al fine*

# Improv Etude - Happy Times

**Module 3**

### Concept: split chords

**Split chords** can occur when playing chords with both hands. A split chord has a bass note in the left hand that is not the root of the chord – sometimes it is not a note from the chord at all.

For example, in m.10 of the Vamp on page 49, you will see an F chord in root position in the right hand with a G as the bass note in the left hand. This is a split chord, written F/G, where the "/" is used to indicate first the chord in the right hand and then the bass note in the left

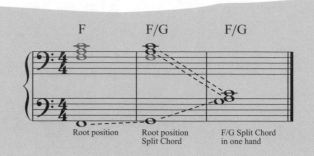

hand. You would say this chord "F over G". In the *Happy Times* improvisation this sound is created in the chord progression by just the left hand.

**A** Label the chord progression with the lettername, (e.g., C7, F7, Dm7, or F/G) and a bracketed number "1" or "3" for the correct inversion. It is common when labelling a chord progression to identify chords only when they are different from the previous chord. Practice the left hand first *without*, then *with* the backing track.

*D.C. al fine*

**B** Tap this rhythm while counting out loud; repeat until memorized. Then tap the rhythm with your right hand while playing the chord progression with your left. Finally, make up your own rhythms to go with the left hand chord progression.

## Improv Tools

There are other Improv Tools you can use to make your improvisation ideas more interesting and musical.

**Pedal Notes**: a pedal note is a repeated note that doesn't change when the melody moves. Here, the C's are pedal notes "above" the melody:

**Idea & Variation**: think of an idea and, using essentially the same notes, play it again with a slight change:

**Chords**: using the Improv Notes, you can also play chords in the right hand for a full, contrasting sound:

**C** Using the Improv Notes Set as indicated in the score, play various right hand improvisations. Use the Improv Tools, above and in the previous Modules, to get started. Practice *with* the backing track.

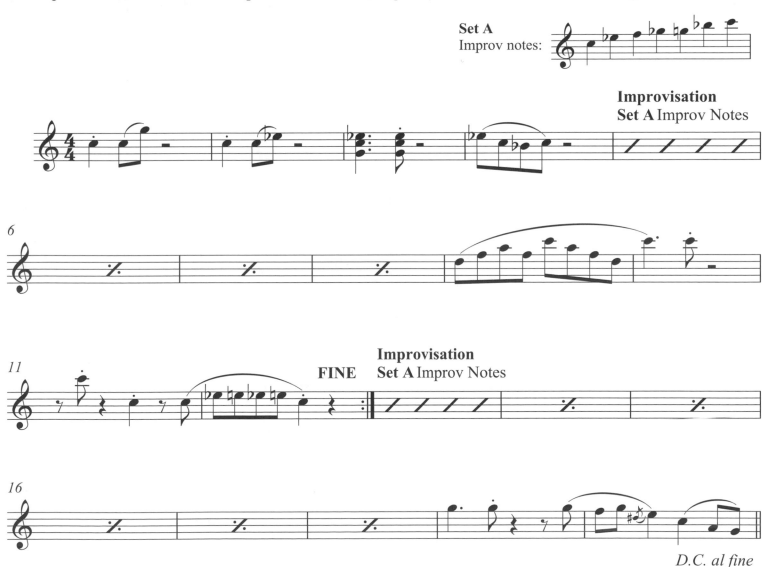

48

**D** Now improvise hands together. Practice first *without*, then *with* the backing track.

*D.C. al fine*

✔ **Improv Tip:** *Begin by making small changes to the melody. Make more changes as you proceed.*

## Vamping Tools

Vamps can also use a mixture of broken and blocked chords. Here are three more effective examples:

Vamp Idea 1 – blocked chords followed by an arpeggio:

Idea 2 – an arpeggio figure followed by blocked chords:

Idea 3 – a variation on Idea 2:

**E** Vamp various right hand accompaniments using the chords [in brackets] indicated below. Use the Vamping Tools, above and in the previous Modules, to get started. Practice first *without*, then *with* the backing track.

*D.C. al fine*

# Improv Etude - To the Stars

**Module 1**

### Concept: split chords

**Split chords** can occur when playing chords with both hands. A split chord has a bass note in the left hand that is not the root of the chord – sometimes it is not a note from the chord at all.

For example, in m.2 of the Vamp on page 53, you will see an E chord in first inversion in the right hand with a B as the bass note in the left hand. This is a split chord, written $E^{(1)}/B$, where the "/" is used to indicate first the chord in the right hand and then the bass note in the left hand. You would say this chord "E over B" or "E one

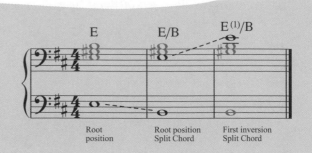

over B". In the *To the Stars* improvisation, the "B" bass note is played in the backing track, creating the split chord sound in relation to the left hand chord.

**A** Label the first inversion split chords with their lettername (e.g., E/B or F♯m/B) and a bracketed 1 for "first inversion", as appropriate. Practice the left hand first *without*, then *with* the backing track.

**B** Tap this rhythm while counting out loud; repeat until memorized. Then tap the rhythm with your right hand while playing the chord progression with your left. Finally, make up your own rhythms to go with the left hand chord progression.

## Improv Tools

To improvise on *To the Stars*, you will use two sets of Improv Notes: one based on the **B minor pentatonic scale**, the other based on the **G Mixolydian mode.**

One way to describe G Mixolydian is as a G Major scale with an F♮ instead of an F♯. Lowering the 7th degree of any major scale by a half step changes it into a Mixolydian mode.

**G Mixolydian mode**

There are Improv Tools you can use to make your improvisation interesting and musical.

**Sequence**: play an idea and then repeat it transposed to start on a different note:

**Direction Change**: play a scale-based idea that changes direction to create contrast:

---

**C** Using the Improv Notes Set A or B as indicated in the score, play various right hand improvisations. Use the Improv Tools, above, to get started. Practice *with* the backing track.

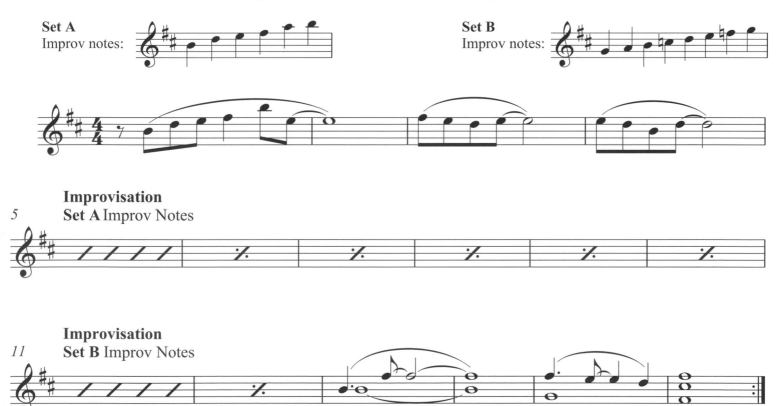

**Set A**
Improv notes:

**Set B**
Improv notes:

**Improvisation**
**Set A** Improv Notes

**Improvisation**
**Set B** Improv Notes

**D** Now improvise hands together. Practice first *without*, then *with* the backing track.

**Improvisation**
**Set A** Improv Notes

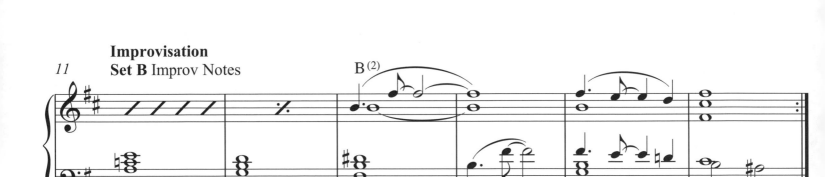

**Improvisation**
**Set B** Improv Notes

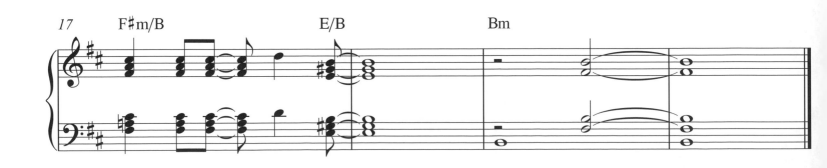

✔ **Improv Tip:** *It's always a good idea to begin simply. Start with a few long notes and gradually become rhythmically busier.*

## Vamping Tools

Vamps can use blocked chords in the right hand. You can create interest by using various rhythmic ideas in both hands:

Vamp Idea 1 – a repeated rhythmic pattern:

Idea 2 – a held chord answered by a syncopated idea:

Idea 3 – a right hand rhythm syncopated to the left hand:

**E** Vamp various right hand accompaniments using the chords [in brackets] indicated below. Use the Vamping Tools, above, to get started. Practice first *without*, then *with* the backing track.

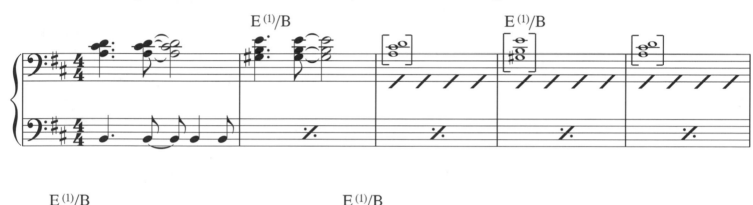

# Improv Etude - To the Stars

**Module 2**

### Concept: minor 7 & minor 9 chords

A **minor 7 chord (m7)** combines a minor triad (e.g., F♯-A-C♯) with a minor 7th above the root (e.g., E). This is the same construction as the 7 chord, only based on a minor triad. Similarly, a **minor 9 chord (m9)** adds a major 9th above the root to the m7 chord.

Minor 7 and 9 chords may be written in **first** and **third inversion**. In a first inversion chord, the third of the chord is on the bottom. In a third inversion chord, the minor seventh of the chord is on the bottom. To review

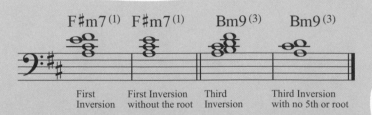

changing root position chords to first or third inversion and three-note voicings, see Modules 1 & 2 of *Heavy Footed* (pp. 14 & 18) and *Clean Sweep* (pp. 26 & 30).

In the *To the Stars* improvisation, the root notes of the m7⁽¹⁾ and m9⁽³⁾ chords are played in the backing track.

**A** Label the first inversion m7 and third inversion m9 chords with their lettername (e.g., F♯m7, Em7, or Bm9) and a bracketed "1" or "3" for the inversion. Practice the left hand first *without*, then *with* the backing track.

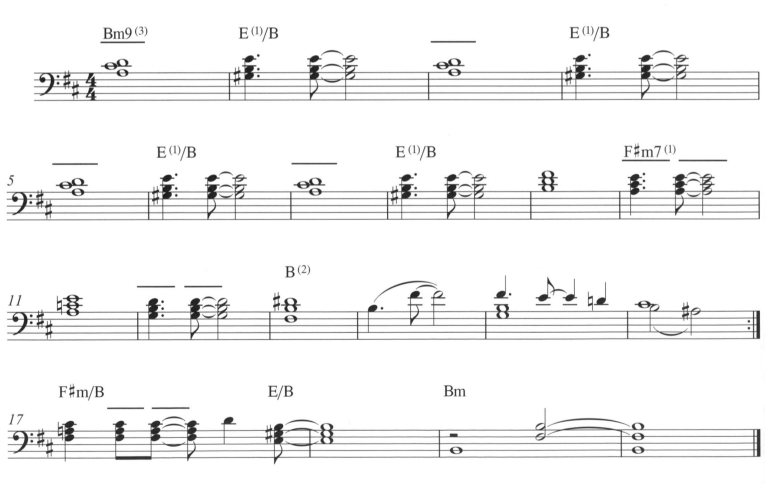

**B** Tap this rhythm while counting out loud; repeat until memorized. Then tap the rhythm with your right hand while playing the chord progression with your left. Finally, make up your own rhythms to go with the left hand chord progression.

## Improv Tools

**Call & Response** is another Improv Tool you can use, in addition to the **Sequence** and **Direction Change**.

**Direction Change**: play an arpeggio-based idea that changes direction to create contrast:

**Sequence**: play an idea and then repeat it transposed to start on a different note:

**Call & Response**: play an arpeggio idea, then "answer" it with a contrasting idea:

**C** Using the Improv Notes Set A or B as indicated in the score, play various right hand improvisations. Use the Improv Tools, above and in the previous Module, to get started. Practice *with* the backing track.

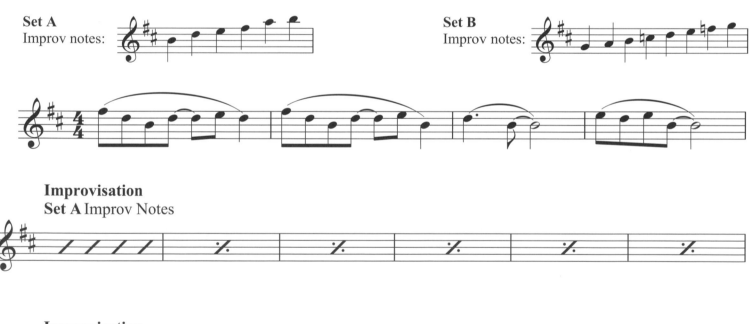

**D** Now improvise hands together. Practice first *without*, then *with* the backing track.

✔ **Improv Tip:** *Try to incorporate rhythmic phrases from the backing track into your improvisation.*

## Vamping Tools

Vamps can use broken chords in the right hand. You can create interest by varying the arpeggio figure:

Idea 2 – start from the top note and move down:

Vamp Idea 1 – start with the bottom note and move up:

Idea 3 – start with the middle note and go either direction:

**E** Vamp various right hand accompaniments using the chords [in brackets] indicated below. Use the Vamping Tools, above and in the previous Module, to get started. Practice first *without*, then *with* the backing track.

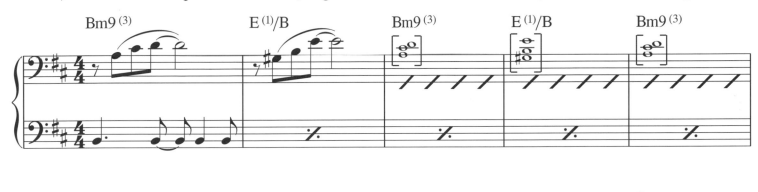

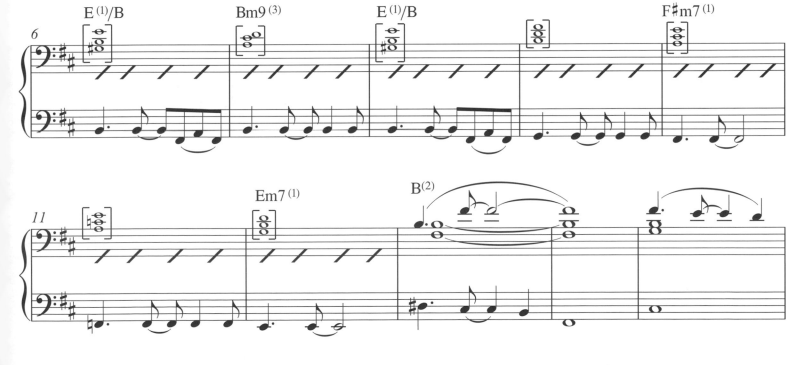

# Improv Etude - To the Stars

**Module 3**

### Concept: major 7 chords

A **major 7 chord (maj7)** combines a major triad (e.g., G-B-D) with a major 7th above the root (e.g., F♯). Notice this is the same construction as the dominant 7 chord, only using a major 7th instead of a minor 7th. Sometimes this is done using all four notes (e.g., G-B-D-F♯), but often it is done using only three notes to achieve the same sound.

Major 7 chords may be written in **root position** and **first inversion**. In a first inversion chord, the third of

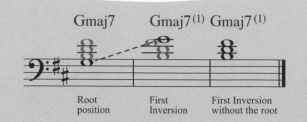

the chord is on the bottom. To review changing root position chords to first inversion and three-note voicings, see Module 1 of *Heavy Footed* (pg. 14) and *Clean Sweep* (pg. 26).

In the *To the Stars* improvisation, the "G" bass note is played in the backing track.

**A** Label the root position and first inversion maj7 chords with their lettername (e.g., Gmaj7 or Fmaj7) and a bracketed 1 for "first inversion", as appropriate. Practice the left hand *without*, then *with* the backing track.

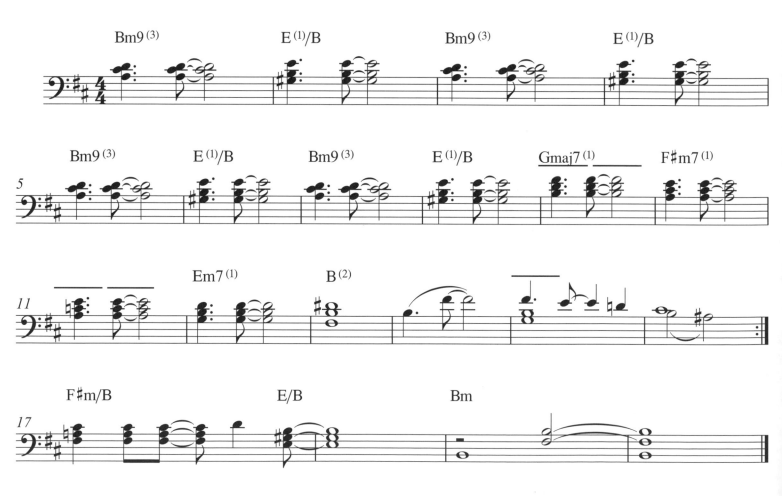

**B** Tap this rhythm while counting out loud; repeat until memorized. Then tap the rhythm with your right hand while playing the chord progression with your left. Finally, make up your own rhythms to go with the left hand chord progression.

## Improv Tools

There are other Improv Tools you can use to make your improvisation ideas more interesting and musical.

**Grace Notes**: grace notes can add expressiveness and a dash of color to your ideas:

**Idea & Variation**: play an idea and then repeat it slightly varied (even by as little as one note!):

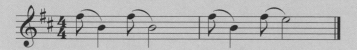

**Chording**: using the Improv Notes, you can also play chords in the right hand for a full, expressive effect:

**C** Using the Improv Notes Set A or B as indicated in the score, play various right hand improvisations. Use the Improv Tools, above and in the previous Modules, to get started. Practice *with* the backing track.

**D** Now improvise hands together. Practice first *without*, then *with* the backing track.

**Set A**
Improv notes:

**Set B**
Improv notes:

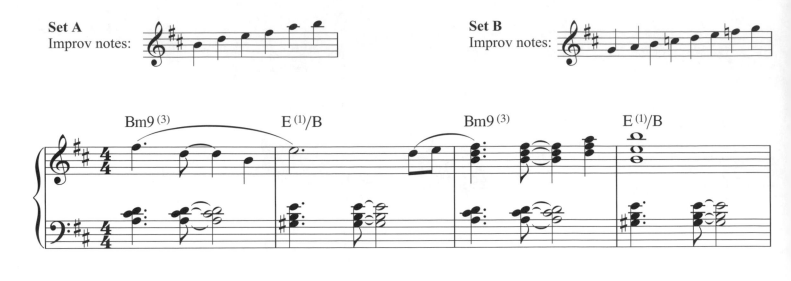

**Improvisation**
**Set A** Improv Notes

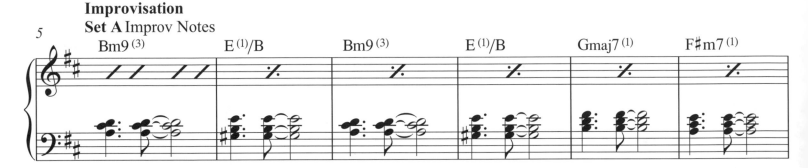

**Improvisation**
**Set B** Improv Notes

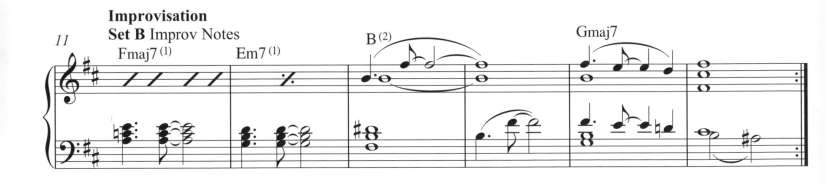

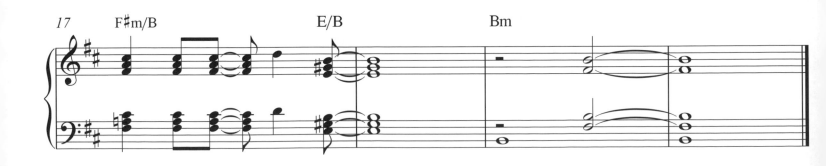

✔ **Improv Tip:** *With a longer improvisation, try to have a plan in mind when you start. Think of your solo as having distinct beginning, middle, and end sections.*

## Vamping Tools

Vamps can use a mixture of blocked and broken chords in the right hand. You can create interest by mixing up the elements – blocked chords, arpeggio figures, and rhythms:

Vamp Idea 1 – arpeggios, held to full chords:

Idea 2 – blocked chords followed by arpeggios:

Idea 3 – arpeggios followed by blocked chords:

**E** Vamp various right hand accompaniments using the chords [in brackets] indicated below. Use the Vamping Tools, above and in the previous Modules, to get started. Practice first *without*, then *with* the backing track.

# Improv Etude - Seaside Town

**Module 1**

### Concept: 9 chords & minor 7 chords

A **9 chord** is a **7 chord** with the 9th scale degree added. A **minor 7 chord (m7)** adds a minor 7th above the root to a minor triad. Often only three notes are used to achieve the same sound of both 9 and m7 chords.

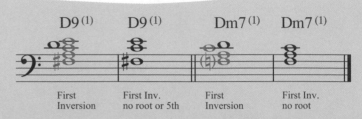

| D9 (1) | D9 (1) | Dm7 (1) | Dm7 (1) |
| First Inversion | First Inv. no root or 5th | First Inversion | First Inv. no root |

Both 9 and minor 7 chords may be written in **first inversion**. In first inversion, the third degree of the scale is on the bottom. To review changing chords to first inversion and three-note voicings, see Modules 1 & 3 of *Heavy Footed* (pp. 14 & 22) and *Clean Sweep* (pp. 26 & 34).

In the *Seaside Town* improvisation, the "D" bass note is played in the backing track. In the Vamp, on page 65, you play it in your left hand.

**A** Label the first inversion 9 and m7 chords with their lettername (e.g., D9, Dm7, or Em7) and a bracketed 1 for "first inversion". Practice the left hand first *without*, then *with* the backing track.

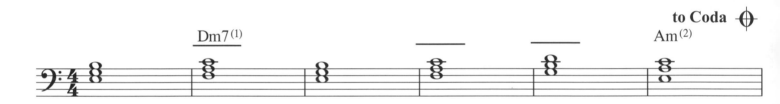

*D.C. al coda*

**B** Tap this rhythm while counting out loud; repeat until memorized. Then tap the rhythm with your right hand while playing the chord progression with your left. Finally, make up your own rhythms to go with the left hand chord progression.

## Improv Tools

Improvisations often use scale-based ideas. To improvise on *Seaside Town*, you will use two different sets of Improv Notes: one based on the **G Mixolydian mode**, the other based on the **A Dorian mode**.

One way to describe A Dorian is as an A **natural minor scale** with an F♯ instead of an F♮. Raising the 6th degree of any natural minor scale changes it into a Dorian mode. To review the G Mixolydian, see *To the Stars* (pg. 51).

There are specific Improv Tools you can use to make your scale-based improvisation interesting and musical.

**Direction Change**: play a scale-based idea and then send it back the other way:

**Sequence**: play a scale-based idea and then repeat it transposed to start on a different note:

**A Dorian mode**

**C** Using the Improv Notes Set A or B as indicated in the score, play various right hand improvisations. Use the Improv Tools, above, to get started. Practice *with* the backing track.

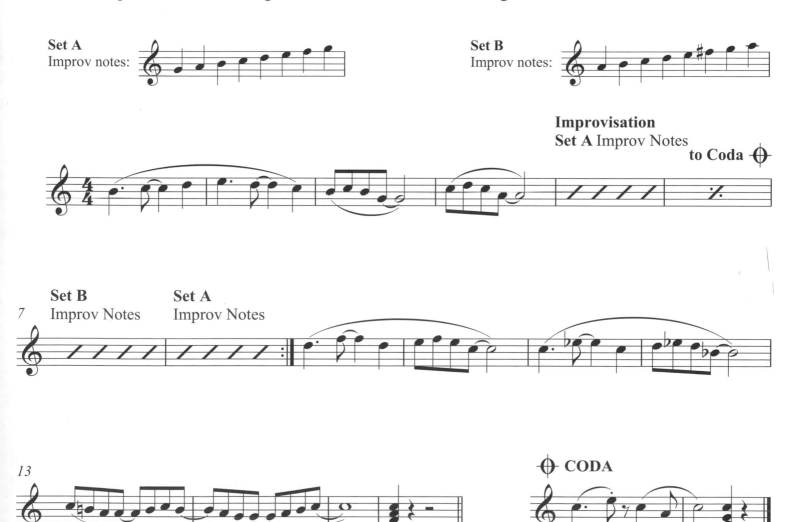

*D.C. al coda*

**D** Now improvise hands together. Practice first *without*, then *with* the backing track.

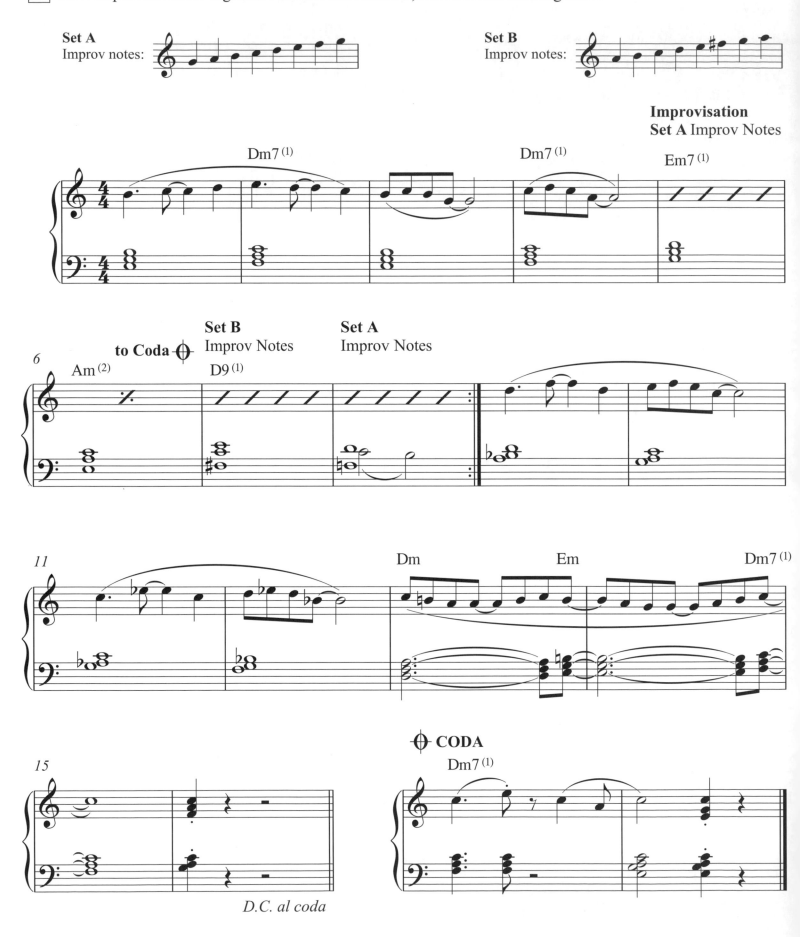

**Improv Tip:** *Varying articulation and dynamics is also part of improvising.  Try it!*

## Vamping Tools

Vamping is an improvised accompaniment style. It often features repeated patterns based on chords in the right hand against single notes in the bass.

You can vary the right hand chords in several ways:

Vamp Idea 1:

Idea 2:

Idea 3:

E  Vamp various right hand accompaniments using the chords [in brackets] indicated below.  Use the Vamping Tools, above, to get started. Practice first *without*, then *with* the backing track.

# Improv Etude - Seaside Town

**Module 2**

### Concept: major 7 chords

A **major 7 chord (maj7)** combines a major triad (e.g., C-E-G) with a major 7 above the root (e.g., B). Often this is done using only three notes to achieve the same sound. Notice this is the same construction as the dominant 7 chord, only using a major 7th above the root instead of a minor 7th.

Major 7 chords may be written in **first inversion**. In a first inversion chord, the third of the chord is on the bottom. To review changing root position chords to first

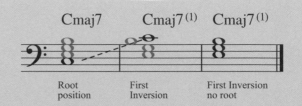

inversion and three-note voicings, see Module 1 of *Heavy Footed* (pg. 14) and *Clean Sweep* (pg. 26).

In the *Seaside Town* improvisation, the "C" bass note is played in the backing track. In the Vamp, on page 69, you play it in your left hand.

**A** Label the first inversion maj7 chords with their lettername (e.g., Cmaj7) and a bracketed 1 for "first inversion". Practice the left hand first *without*, then *with* the backing track.

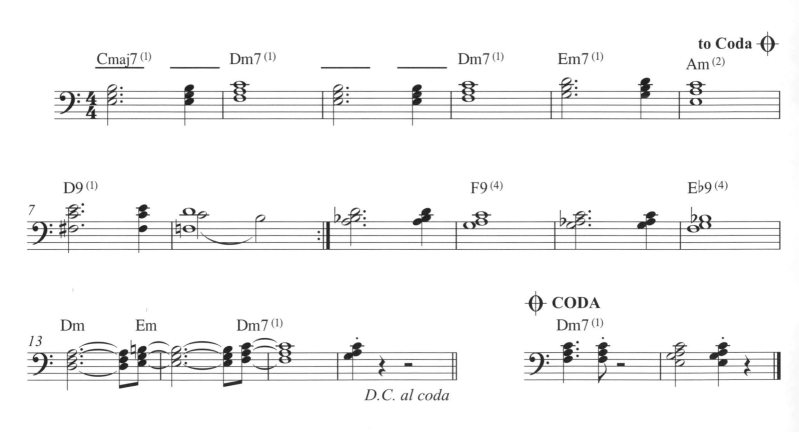

**B** Tap this rhythm while counting out loud; repeat until memorized. Then tap the rhythm with your right hand while playing the chord progression with your left. Finally, make up your own rhythms to go with the left hand chord progression.

## Improv Tools

Improvisations can use arpeggio-based ideas. **Octave Transposition** is another Tool you can use, in addition to the **Direction Change** and **Sequence** Tools.

**Sequence**: play an arpeggio-based idea and then repeat it transposed to start on a different note:

**Direction Change**: play an arpeggio-based idea and then change its direction:

**Octave Transposition**: play an arpeggio-based idea and then repeat it transposed up an octave:

**C** Using the Improv Notes Set A or B as indicated in the score, play various right hand improvisations. Use the Improv Tools, above and in the previous Module, to get started. Practice *with* the backing track.

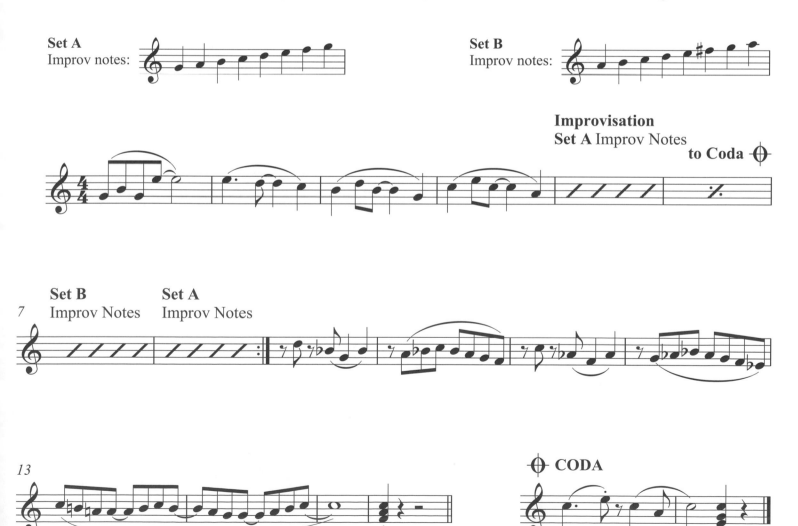

**D** Now improvise hands together. Practice first *without*, then *with* the backing track.

*D.C. al coda*

✔ **Improv Tip:** *Try using all scale-based ideas, then all arpeggio-based ideas to get a feel for the different sound.*

## Vamping Tools

Vamps can use broken chords in the right hand. You can create interest by varying the arpeggio figure:

Vamp Idea 1 – start with the bottom note and move up:

Idea 2 – start from the top note and move down:

Idea 3 – start with the middle note and go either direction:

**E** Vamp various right hand accompaniments using the chords [in brackets] indicated below. Use the Vamping Tools, above and in the previous Module, to get started. Practice first *without*, then *with* the backing track.

*D.C. al coda*

# Improv Etude - Seaside Town

**Module 3**

## Concept: split chords

**Split chords** can occur when playing chords with both hands. A split chord has a bass note in the left hand that is not the root of the chord – sometimes it is not a note from the chord at all.

For example, in m.9 of the Vamp on page 73, you will see a B♭maj7 chord in third inversion in the right hand with a C as the bass note in the left hand. This is a split chord, written B♭maj7$^{(3)}$/C, where the "/" is used to indicate first the chord in the right hand and then the bass note in the left hand. You would say this chord

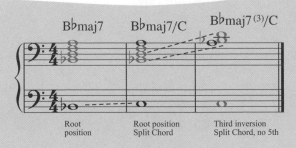

"B♭ major 7 over C" or "B♭ major 7 three over C".

In the *Seaside Town* improvisation, the "C" bass note is omitted from the left hand chord progression; the split chord sound is created by the bass part in the backing track.

**A** Label the third inversion split chords with their lettername (e.g., B♭maj7/C) and a bracketed 3 for "third inversion". Practice the left hand first *without*, then *with* the backing track.

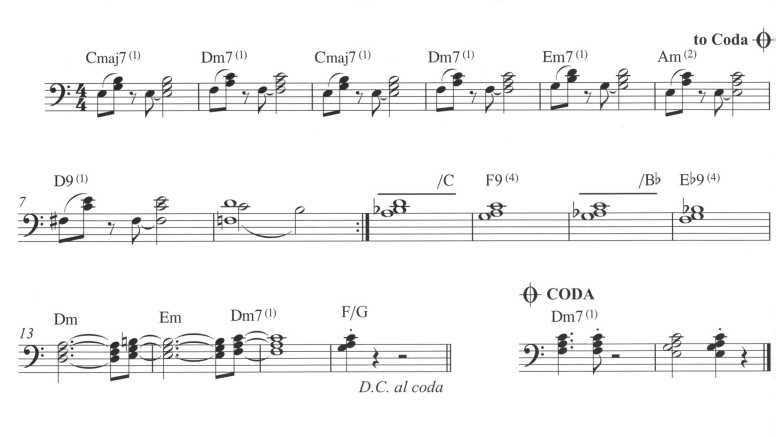

**B** Tap this rhythm while counting out loud; repeat until memorized. Then tap the rhythm with your right hand while playing the chord progression with your left. Finally, make up your own rhythms to go with the left hand chord progression.

## Improv Tools

There are various other things you can use to make your improvisation more interesting and exciting.

**Thirds**: play your musical idea in thirds to add further expressiveness to a melody:

**Grace Notes**: grace notes can give your improvisation character:

**Pedal Notes**: a pedal note is a repeated note that doesn't change when the melody moves. Here, the G's are pedal notes "above" the melody:

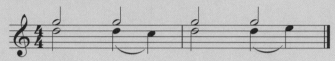

**C** Using the Improv Notes Set A or B as indicated in the score, play various right hand improvisations. Use the Improv Tools, above and in the previous Modules, to get started. Practice *with* the backing track.

**D** Now improvise hands together. Practice first *without*, then *with* the backing track.

*D.C. al coda*

✔ **Improv Tip:** *See how many different ways you can use pedal notes above the melody.*

## Vamping Tools

Vamps can use a mixture of blocked and arpeggiated chords in the right hand. You can create interest by mixing up the elements – blocked chords, arpeggio figures, and rhythms:

Vamp Idea 1 – a syncopated chord idea followed by arpeggios:

Idea 2 – arpeggios followed by a syncopated chord idea:

Idea 3 – full chords followed by arpeggios:

E  Vamp various right hand accompaniments using the chords [in brackets] indicated below. Use the Vamping Tools, above and in the previous Modules, to get started. Practice first *without*, then *with* the backing track.

# Andante

Félix Le Couppey

*D.C. al fine*

# Allegretto

J.B. Duvernoy

# Grazioso

Alexander Goedicke

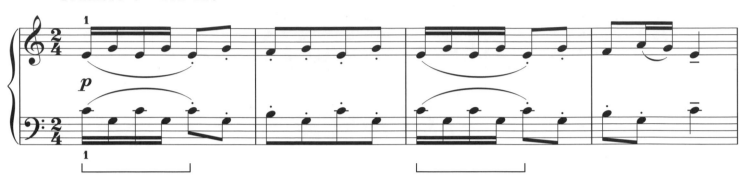

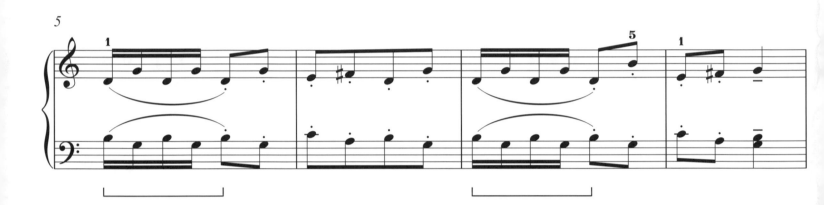

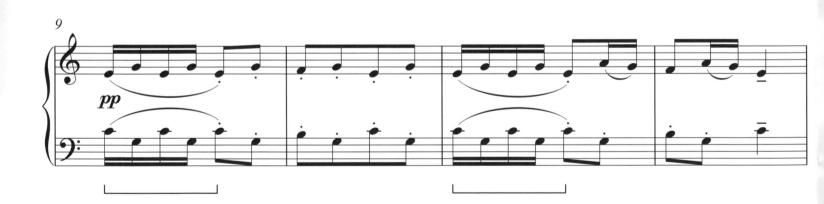

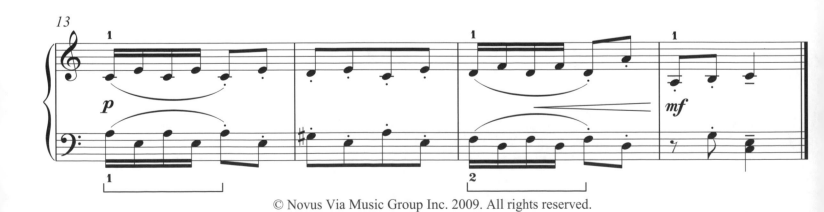

# Moderato

Henri-Jerome Bertini

# Moderato

Stephen Heller

# Marziale

Carl Czerny

# Snowflakes

Christopher Norton

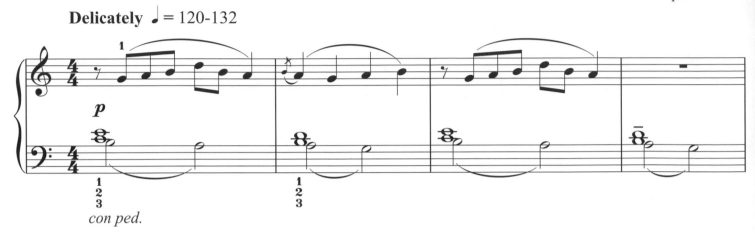

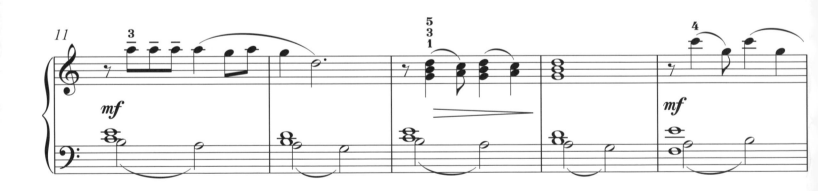

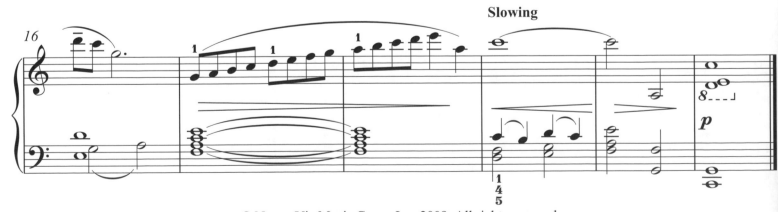

# For a Split Second

Christopher Norton

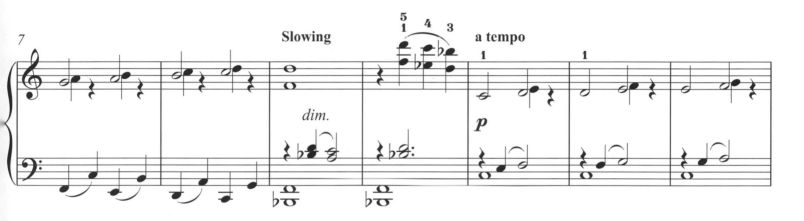

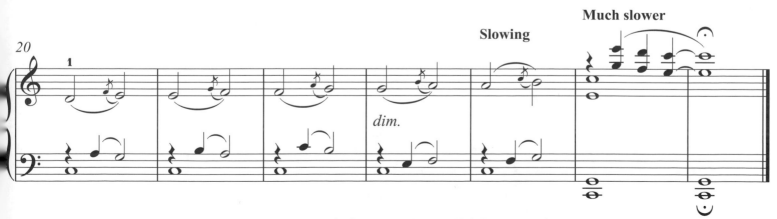

# At the Ready

Christopher Norton

# Across the Beat

Christopher Norton

# Five to Three

Christopher Norton

# Touching the Light

Christopher Norton

# LEVEL 6 ETUDES

## Glossary

## Chord Structures

**6 Chords** ...... Chords which contain the sixth scale degree above the root.

major 6 ...... Combines a major triad (C-E-G) with the note a major sixth above the root (A). Notated: C6

minor 6 ...... Combines a minor triad (C-E♭-G) with the note a major sixth above the root (A). Notated: Cm6

**7 Chords** ...... Chords which contain either a major or minor seventh scale degree above the root.

dominant 7 .. Also known as a "7 chord". A major triad (C-E-G) combined with the note a minor 7th above the root (B♭). Notated: C7

major 7 ...... Combines a major triad (C-E-G) with the note a major seventh above the root (B). Notated: Cmaj7

minor 7 ...... A minor triad (C-E♭-G) combined with the note a minor seventh above the root (B♭). Notated: Cm7

**9 Chords** ...... Extended chords which contain the major ninth scale degree above the root

dominant 9 .. Also known as a "9 chord". A 7 chord (C-E-G-B♭) with an added major ninth on top (C-E-G-B♭-D). Notated: C9

major 9 ...... Adds a ninth above the root to the maj7 chord (C-E-G-B-D). Notated: Cmaj9

minor 9 ...... A minor 7 chord (C-E♭-G-B♭) with an added major ninth above the root (D). Notated: Cm9

**13 Chords** ..... Extended chords which contain the major 13th scale degree above the root.

dominant 13 . Also known as a "13 chord". A 7 chord (C-E-G-B♭) with an added major 9th, 11th, and 13th above the root (D, F, A an octave above). Usually the 11th and sometimes the 9th are omitted. Notated: C13

**Add Chords** .. Indicates a note above the octave is added to a non-7 chord, without including every chord note in between. See Extended Chords.

add9 .......... Starts with a triad (C-E-G) and adds the note a ninth above the root (D). Notated: Cadd9

m6add9 ...... Starts with a m6 chord (C-E♭-G-A) and adds a ninth above the root to the chord (D). Notated: Cm6add9

**Augmented Chords** ... A major chord in which the fifth is raised a half step (C-E-G♯). Notated: Caug

7aug .......... A 7 chord in which the fifth is raised a half step (C-E-G♯-B♭). Notated: C7aug

**Close Position** ........... When the notes of a chord are arranged as close together as possible (C major triad played C-E-G).

**Extended Chords** ...... Indicates a note or notes above the octave are added to a 7 chord; could include every chord note in between (9, 11, or 13 chords). See Added Chords.

**Inversions** ..... Chords in which the root is not on the bottom.

first .......... The third of a chord (the note E in a C major chord of C) is at the bottom of a chord (E-G-C). Notated: C[1]

second ....... The fifth of a chord (the note G in a C major chord of C) is at the bottom of a chord (G-C-E). Notated: C[2]

third .......... The seventh of a chord (the note B♭ in a C7 chord) is at the bottom of a chord (B♭-C-E-G). Notated: C7[3]

fourth ........ When the ninth of a chord (the note D in a C9 chord) is at the bottom of a chord (D-E-G-B♭-C). Notated: C9[4]

**Root Position** ........... When a chord is written line-line-line (line-line) or space-space-space (space-space), it is in root position. The root is the bottom note.

**Split Chords** .. Chords which contain a bass note which is not the root of the chord. Often the bass note is not a note from the chord at all.

major 7 ...... Puts a maj7 chord in the right hand (C-E-G-B) over a bass note in the left hand, usually down at least one octave, other than the root (D). Notated: Cmaj7/D

major 6 ...... Combines a maj6 chord in the right hand (C-E-G-A) over a bass note in the left hand, usually down at least one octave, other than the root (D). Notated: C6/D

**Sus4 Chords** .. Also known as a "sus" chord. When a triad is written using the fourth degree of the scale instead of the third, the fourth is said to be "suspending" the expected resolution to the third.

7sus .......... Raises the third of a 7 chord to the fourth (C-F-G-B♭). Notated: C7sus

## Melodic Structures

**Blues scale** .... A six-note blues scale consists of a minor pentatonic scale with the addition of a flatted fifth (or sharpened fourth) scale degree (C-E♭-F-G♭-G-B♭).

**Modes** ........ Scales with names drawn from the ancient Greeks, used in folk, pop, and some classical pieces.

Dorian ....... A seven-note scale with half steps between scale degrees 2-3 and 6-7 (C-D-E♭-F-G-A-B♭-C).

Lydian ....... A seven-note scale with half steps between scale degrees 4-5 and 7-8 (C-D-E-F♯-G-A-B-C).

Mixolydian .. A seven-note scale with half steps between scale degrees 3-4 and 6-7 (C-D-E-F-G-A-B♭-C).

Phrygian ..... A seven-note scale with half steps between scale degrees 1-2 and 5-6 (C-D♭-E♭-F-G-A♭-B♭-C).

**Pentatonic** .... A five-note scale based on the first five notes of the overtone series (C-G-D-A-E), arranged in scale form (C-D-E-G-A).

major .......... A common form of this five-note scale uses scale degrees 1-2-3-5-6 of a major scale (C-D-E-G-A).

minor ........ A common form of this five-note scale uses scale degrees 1-3-4-5-7 of a natural minor scale (C-E♭-F-G-B♭).

## Terms & Symbols

**Calypso** ........ A form derived from African and Caribbean folk music. Usually in duple meter, with syncopated rhythms.

**Licks** ........... Short, catchy melodic motifs, often used to describe guitar playing.

**Motif** .......... A group of notes that form a musical idea.

**Ostinato** ....... A rhythmic or melodic pattern repeated at length in one voice.

**Repeat**

full bar ....... Repeat the entire previous measure.

double full bar ....... repeat the entire previous two measures.

**Riff** ............. Another term for ostinato, often used in pop music. A repeated pattern of notes, chord progression, or rhythmic pattern, often played by the rhythm section.

**Slash notation** ........... Signals performers to create their own rhythmic pattern. A slash is placed over each beat.

**Tremolo** ....... A fast alternation between two notes, notated by strokes on the stem of the notes, or between the stems of the notes.